How does it work?

Dorling DK Kindersley

LONDON, NEW YORK, SYDNEY, DELHI, PARIS,
MUNICH, and JOHANNESBURG

Project Editors: Angela Wilkes, Judith Hodge, Jane Yorke
Project Art Editors: Michelle Baxter, Helen Melville
Senior Editor: Sarah Levete
Editors: Dawn Rowley, Anna Lofthouse
Senior Art Editors: Chris Scollen, Adrienne Hutchinson
Art Editor: Emy Manby
Managing Editors: Linda Martin, Mary Atkinson
Managing Art Editor: Peter Bailey
Senior DTP Designer: Bridget Roseberry
Production: Erica Rosen
Picture Researchers: Louise Thomas, Frances Vargo, Andrea Sadler
Computer-generated artwork: Alternative View
Photography: Steve Gorton, Gary Ombler
Jacket Designers: Karen Burgess, Sophia Tampakopoulos

First American Edition, 2001
00 01 02 03 04 05 10 9 8 7 6 5 4 3 2 1

Published in the United States by Dorling Kindersley Publishing, Inc.
95 Madison Avenue, New York, New York 10016

A Cataloging-in-Publication record is available from the Library of Congress

ISBN 0-7894-1252-5

Color reproduction by Colourscan, Singapore
Printed and bound in Italy by L.E.G.O.

The publisher would like to thank the following for their kind permission to reproduce their photographs:
a=above; c=center; b=below; l=left; r=right; t=top

Allsport: Vandystadt 47br; **© Alton Towers:** 111tl; **Corbis UK Ltd:** Julie Houck 37tl; **Corbis UK Ltd:** 63bl; **Corbis UK Ltd:** 101tl, 107tl; **Dale Buckton:** 29tr; **Robert Harding Picture Library:** Steve Myerson 27tl; **Adrienne Hutchinson:** 19br;

Image Bank: Steve Dunwell 23tl; **Images Colour Library:** 77tl, 83t; **Photofusion:** Ray Roberts 89tl; **Pictor International:** 53t; **Pictor International:** 97tr; **Pictor International:** 80-81, 87cr; **Redferns:** Nicky J. Sims 104tr; **Rex Features:** 31tl; **Rex Features:** 103tl; Peter Brooker 21tl; **Science Photo Library:** European Space Agency 71tc; **The Stock Market:** 48b, 55t; J. Marshall 57tl; **The Stock Market:** 97tc; Michael A. Keller Studios 1999; **Tony Stone Images:** Nicole Katano 45br;

Warren Bolster 61b; **Tony Stone Images:** John Lund 79tl; Mike Abrahams 75tr; **Tony Stone Images:** Chris Shim 115tl; **Telegraph Colour Library:** 73tl; **Telegraph Colour Library:** Stephen Simpson 109tc; **Art Directors & TRIP:** J. Drew 85tl.

see our complete catalog at **www.dk.com**

Experiments in
Science

How does it work?

written by David Glover

A Dorling Kindersley Book

Contents

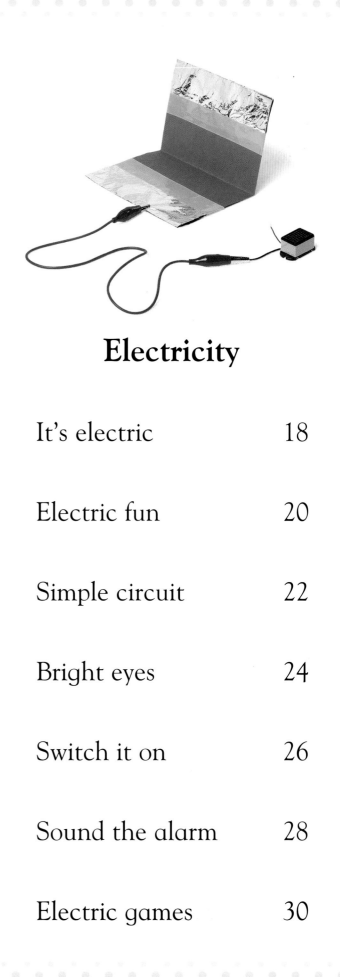

Electricity

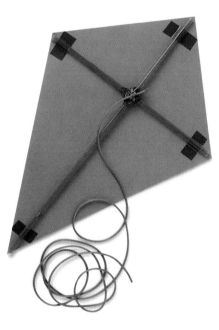

Forces and Movement

Light and Color

Sound and Music

Hello!

Meet Chip, Pixel, and their helpful dog, Newton. Join these three friendly characters as they take you on an exciting and fact-filled journey of scientific discovery.

I'm Chip!

I'm Pixel!

Grrrr, I'm Newton!

Before you begin
You'll need an adult to help you with the experiments in this book. Before starting, read the introduction, the list of equipment, and the instructions. Make sure you look at the numbers on the instructions – they'll help you follow the steps one by one.

After reading the instructions, try to work out what you think will happen. After the experiment, think back to what you predicted. Did it happen as you expected?

Your scientific equipment
Look for the box like this by each experiment. Inside, you'll find a list of all the equipment you'll need – but remember to ask an adult before you use anything.

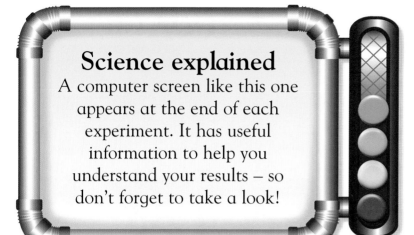

Science explained

A computer screen like this one appears at the end of each experiment. It has useful information to help you understand your results – so don't forget to take a look!

Extra information

At the back of the book, you'll find a glossary that tells you the meanings of new words. There's also an index to help you find your way around the book.

Science in real life

For each experiment, there's a photo showing a real-life example of the science that you're investigating. Can you think of any more real-life examples?

For your helper

Each section of this book has parents' notes especially for the adult who's helping you. The parents' notes for Electricity are on pages 16–17, Forces and Movement are on pages 42–43, Light and Color are on pages 68–69, and Sound and Music are on pages 94–95.

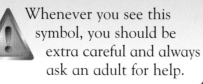

Get experimenting and have fun!

Test your knowledge

When you've finished all the experiments in each section, find out how much you remember by doing the fun quiz at the end.

Science safety

Science experiments are fun, but you still need to be careful. Read through the instructions with an adult to see where you might need help.

Be especially careful when using any sharp tools, such as scissors. Always use round-ended scissors and, if necessary, ask an adult to help you.

Whenever you see this symbol, you should be extra careful and always ask an adult for help.

Electricity

Parents' notes

This section will help your child to develop a basic understanding of the sources of electricity and how electrical circuits make things work. Read these notes and any on the relevant pages to help your child get the most out of the experiments.

Pages 18–19: It's electric

Discuss with your child the difference between household current (AC) and battery electricity (DC) and help him or her to find everyday electrical appliances around the home. It is very important to talk with your child about the dangers of electricity.

Pages 20–21: Electric fun

Here your child will learn about batteries as a source of power. Emphasize that batteries have a limited supply of electricity whereas there is a continuous supply from the wall outlet. You may need to help your child remove and insert the batteries and look for the positive and negative signs.

Pages 22–23: Simple circuit*

Punch a hole in the base of the tube. Make sure your child recognizes that when the bulb lights up, the circuit is complete. Point out the similarity between the words *circuit* and *circle* to help your child see that all the parts must connect in a loop to allow the flow of electricity.

Pages 24–25: Bright eyes

You might like to make a one-eyed monster first, and then add the other eye. This would show that two bulbs in a circuit glow dimmer than one bulb because it is more difficult for the electricity to flow through two bulbs one after the other. Your child may need help cutting out the face and mouth of the monster.

Pages 26–27: Switch it on

On these pages, your child will learn that switches have a dual purpose – they can connect circuits and can break them. As soon as a circuit has a break in it (when the switch is turned off), the electricity is unable to flow.

Pages 28–29: Sound the alarm

This activity incorporates a buzzer in a simple circuit. Explain to your child that the aluminum foil acts as a switch because aluminum is an electrical conductor – a material that allows electricity to flow through it.

Pages 30–31: Electric games

Help your child to bend the wire into a wiggly shape and to make a ring. Check that the objects in the circuit are connected correctly, otherwise the buzzer will not sound. When the ring touches the wire, it is effectively turning on a switch. You could use a bulb that lights up when the circuit is connected as an alternative to the buzzer.

Pages 32–33: Code tapper

This circuit also needs a switch to make it complete – the paper clip-and-button tapper. Make sure that the glue attaching the button to the paper clip does not cover the wire that touches the thumbtack. Your child can have fun devising a special code to send a secret message.

Pages 34–35: Electric fan

Here your child will learn that electric power can make things move, for example, the spindle on the motor that makes the propeller spin. Make sure that your child does not touch the propeller when it is rotating.

Pages 36–37: Electric tester

This fun test will help your child understand that some materials let electricity pass through them (conductors) while others don't (insulators). Make sure the two wires on the object being tested do not touch. Ask your child to describe the materials that the insulators and conductors are made of.

* This experiment shows how to make a simple circuit. From pages 22–23 onward, many of the experiments include simple circuits. The wires used throughout the book come with crocodile clips already attached. There are additional instructions on pages 22–23 explaining how to attach wires without crocodile clips.

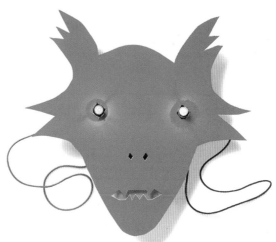

It's electric

Lights, heaters, and many machines run on electricity. Some things use household current, which comes from power stations to your home. Others use electricity stored in batteries. How many things in your home can you find that run on electricity?

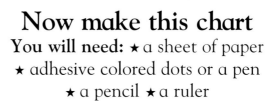

Woof woof

Now make this chart
You will need: ★ a sheet of paper ★ adhesive colored dots or a pen ★ a pencil ★ a ruler

On the move
Radios and CD players can often run on both household current and electricity from batteries. You don't need to be near an outlet to turn on a radio that is running on batteries. This means that you can listen to a radio wherever you are.

ruler

pencil

1 Draw a chart with three columns on the sheet of paper. In the first column, list all the different electric things you can find in your house.

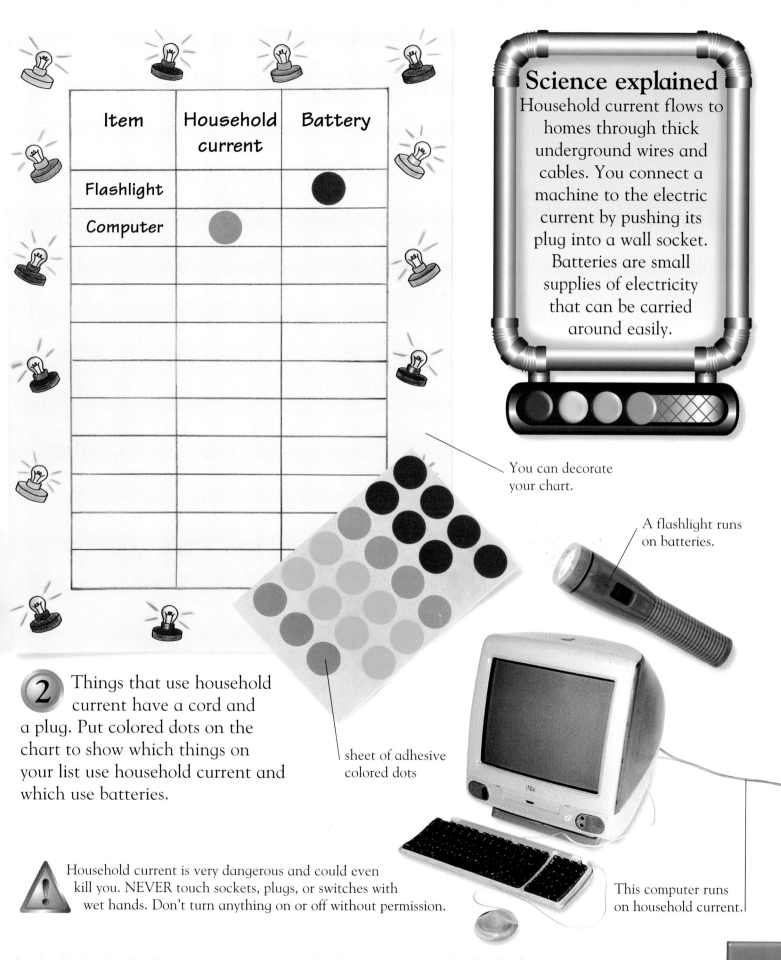

Item	Household current	Battery
Flashlight		●
Computer	●	

Science explained

Household current flows to homes through thick underground wires and cables. You connect a machine to the electric current by pushing its plug into a wall socket. Batteries are small supplies of electricity that can be carried around easily.

You can decorate your chart.

A flashlight runs on batteries.

sheet of adhesive colored dots

2 Things that use household current have a cord and a plug. Put colored dots on the chart to show which things on your list use household current and which use batteries.

This computer runs on household current.

Household current is very dangerous and could even kill you. NEVER touch sockets, plugs, or switches with wet hands. Don't turn anything on or off without permission.

Electric fun

Have you got any toys or other small machines that run on electricity? Most electric toys have batteries inside them that make them work. The electricity gives the toys the power to do lots of different things.

Now find out more
You will need: ★ several battery-operated toys and other items, such as flashlights or calculators

battery

battery case

Match up the signs, + and –, and put the batteries back in the case.

1 Ask an adult to help you open the battery cases of different toys. Look at the size of the battery each toy uses, and how many batteries each toy needs.

2 Look at the batteries and the inside of the battery case. Can you see the plus signs (+) and minus signs (–) at the ends of each battery? Match the signs on the batteries with the signs on the case.

Science explained

A battery contains chemicals that make electricity. You must match the + and – signs on the battery and the case so the electricity can flow. Batteries do not last forever. After awhile, they run out of electricity, and the toy stops working. Then you have to put in new batteries.

Electric car

Some cars run on electricity instead of gasoline. They have powerful batteries that make them work.

Whoosh

3 When you put batteries in a toy or a small machine, it may not work right away. What happens if you flick the switch?

switch

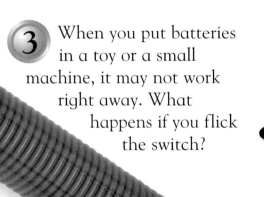

4 What do the batteries in each toy make it do? Does it light up, move, or make a sound? Can you think of any other things that toys with batteries can do?

This battery-operated toy can do addition for you.

Simple circuit

Inside electric machines there are often bulbs, switches, and other electric parts. For the machine to work, all these parts must be joined together by wires to make a ring called a circuit. Try making this model with a simple circuit.

Now make a model lighthouse
You will need: ★ a clear, plastic cup ★ a cardboard tube with a lid ★ a bulb in a bulb holder ★ a battery ★ 2 wires ★ adhesive tape

1 Take the lid off the tube. Ask an adult to punch a hole in the base of the tube. Thread two wires through the hole.

hole in base of tube

wire with crocodile clip

bulb in bulb holder

adhesive tape

If your wires do not have crocodile clips, strip the plastic from the end of each wire and twist the bare wire around each screw.

2 Connect one end of each wire to each of the screws on the bulb holder. Tape the bulb holder onto the base of the tube.

Science explained

The battery, wires, and bulb make a complete circuit. Electricity from the battery flows along one wire to the bulb, then back to the battery along the other wire. The moving electricity lights up the bulb. If you disconnect one wire, you break the circuit and electricity stops moving.

Powerful light

This lighthouse shines brightly in the dark to warn sailors that they are sailing near a rocky area. The light is powered by electricity.

 Ask an adult to strip the ends of the wires for you.

Tape the cup onto the tube to make it look like a real lighthouse.

The circuit is now complete and the bulb lights up.

3 Connect the other end of each wire to the battery. Place the battery on the inside of the tube lid.

Clip the wires to the battery, or hold the bare end in place using adhesive tape.

tube lid

4 Put the tube over the battery and press it firmly onto the lid. Tape the plastic cup over the bulb. To turn off the bulb, take off the lid, and disconnect one wire from the battery.

Decorate your lighthouse with stripes of adhesive tape.

Bright eyes

You can connect more than one bulb into an electric circuit. Try making this circuit to see if you can light two bulbs with just one battery to make a model monster's eyes glow in the dark.

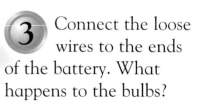

Now make a monster
You will need: ★ 2 bulbs in bulb holders ★ 3 wires ★ a battery ★ colored cardboard ★ colored paper ★ scissors ★ adhesive tape ★ nontoxic glue

1 Attach a wire to each of the screws on one bulb holder.

2 Connect the other end of one of these wires to the second bulb holder. Connect your third wire to the other screw on the second bulb holder.

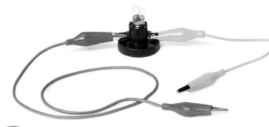

This wire connects to the second bulb holder.

The circuit is now complete.

3 Connect the loose wires to the ends of the battery. What happens to the bulbs?

Linking lights

The bulbs of Christmas tree lights are all connected by wires and plugged into a socket. If one bulb stops working, all the others stop working, too.

Tape the bulb holders to the back of the face.

Tape the battery in place.

monster face cut out of green cardboard

bulbs for eyes

glue on the mouth and nose

4 Ask an adult to cut the cardboard into a monster face with two eye holes. Push the bulbs through the holes in the back of the cardboard. Tape the bulbs and the battery onto the back of the cardboard.

5 Turn the monster face around. Finish it by gluing on a paper mouth and nose. Watch the eyes glow!

Switch it on

At the flick of a switch, your room fills with light. When you switch on the TV, pictures and sounds appear. Most electrical things have a switch. Try making a tiny lamp you can switch on and off.

Now make a lamp with a switch

You will need: ★ a large, metal paper clip ★ 2 metal thumbtacks ★ a small block of wood ★ 3 wires ★ a battery ★ a bulb in a bulb holder ★ nontoxic glue ★ a clear, plastic cup ★ colored tissue paper

1 Ask an adult to attach one end of a wire to the top of a thumbtack.

thumbtack

Place the thumbtack so that the paper clip can swing around to touch it.

This is your switch.

2 Put the paper clip on the wood. Push the thumbtack through one end of the paper clip so that it can turn.

paper clip held in place by thumbtack

3 Attach another wire to the second thumbtack, and push the thumbtack into the wood. Make sure the paper clip can touch the thumbtack when you turn it.

Night lights

As soon as it gets dark in the evening, people flick the switches in their homes and offices to turn on the lights. Think how much electricity is being used!

Glue colored tissue paper around the cup to decorate it.

5 Put the cup over the bulb to complete your lamp. How do you switch off the lamp?

wire from bulb to battery

battery

4 Connect the switch to one end of the battery and to the bulb holder. Connect the bulb holder to the battery with another wire.

wire from switch to bulb

wire from switch to battery

The switch is on when the paper clip touches both thumbtacks.

Sound the alarm

A burglar breaks in, empty bag ready, but he steps on a hidden switch and sets off the alarm! The police are on their way! Try guarding your bedroom by making this alarm. It sets off a buzzer with a simple switch.

Now make a burglar alarm
You will need: ★ a rectangular piece of stiff cardboard ★ aluminum foil ★ a buzzer ★ a battery ★ 3 wires ★ adhesive tape

adhesive tape

folded cardboard

aluminum foil

wire connected to foil

buzzer

1 Fold the cardboard in half. Cover the ends of the cardboard with aluminum foil, leaving a gap along the fold. Tape the foil in place.

2 Attach one end of a wire to the foil on the cardboard. Connect the other end of the wire to the buzzer.

3 Use another wire to connect the buzzer to the battery. Connect the other end of the cardboard to the battery.

This circuit with a buzzer forms the alarm.

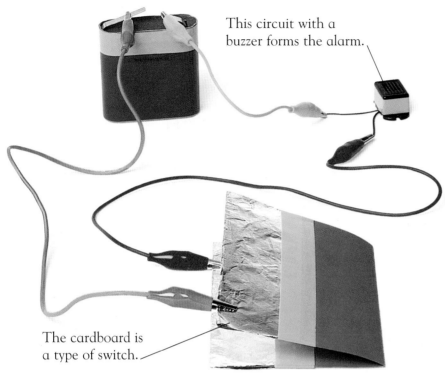

The cardboard is a type of switch.

Ringing bells
When you ring on the doorbell of a friend's house, you press a button. This turns on a switch that completes a circuit to make the bell ring.

4 Hide the alarm near a door so that when the door opens the two foil-covered ends of the cardboard switch are pushed together. Try it yourself. What happens?

The foil-covered ends of the cardboard must touch each other to turn the switch on.

Science explained
The foil-covered cardboard is a switch. Electricity can flow through the aluminum foil. When the foil ends of the cardboard are pushed together, the switch is on and the electric circuit is complete. Electricity flows around it and makes the buzzer go off.

29

Electric games

At a fairground, lights flash, bells ring, and dodgem cars crash. Many games and rides run on electricity and are turned on by different types of switches. Try making an electric game of your own to test your skills.

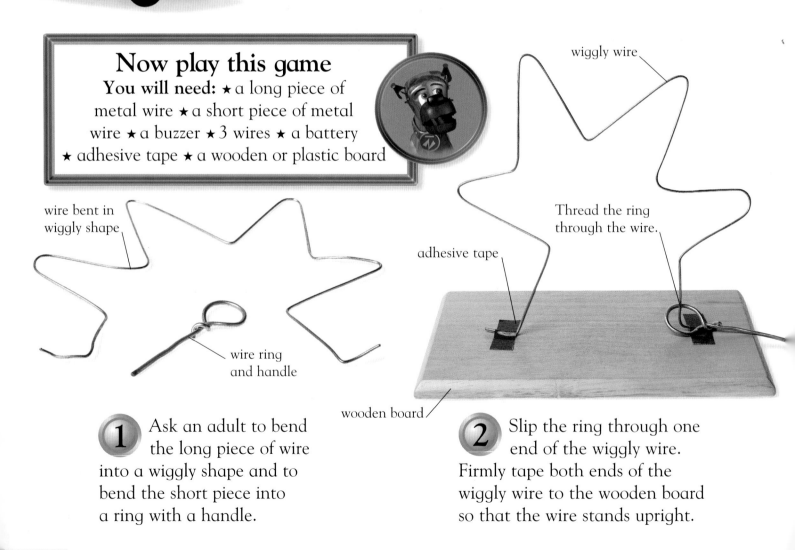

Now play this game
You will need: ★ a long piece of metal wire ★ a short piece of metal wire ★ a buzzer ★ 3 wires ★ a battery ★ adhesive tape ★ a wooden or plastic board

wiggly wire

wire bent in wiggly shape

Thread the ring through the wire.

adhesive tape

wire ring and handle

wooden board

1 Ask an adult to bend the long piece of wire into a wiggly shape and to bend the short piece into a ring with a handle.

2 Slip the ring through one end of the wiggly wire. Firmly tape both ends of the wiggly wire to the wooden board so that the wire stands upright.

Pressing the pedal

What makes a dodgem car move? The foot pedal is a switch. When you press the switch, it turns on the electricity, which travels down a pole to power the dodgem car.

3 Use two wires to connect the buzzer to one end of the battery and to the wiggly wire. Use the third wire to connect the wire ring to the other end of the battery.

4 Try moving the ring from one end of the wiggly wire to the other without touching it. What happens if the ring touches the wire?

Buzz

This wire connects the wire ring to the battery.

This wire connects the buzzer to the battery.

buzzer

This wire connects the buzzer to the wiggly wire.

Code tapper

Messages can be sent using electricity. When you speak on the telephone, electric signals carry the sound of your voice to the person you are talking to. Try making an electric tapper to send secret messages in code!

Now make a code tapper
You will need: ★ 2 metal thumbtacks ★ glue ★ a large, metal paper clip ★ a small block of wood ★ adhesive tape ★ a buzzer ★ a battery ★ a plastic button ★ 3 wires

1 Ask an adult to help you make a switch with a paper clip and thumbtacks, as shown on page 26. Tape the short part of the paper clip to the wood.

thumbtack

short part of paper clip taped to wood

block of wood

2 Bend the long end of the paper clip upward. Glue the button to the end of the paper clip.

long end of paper clip

button

buzzer connected to two wires

button switch

3 Connect two wires to the buzzer. Connect one of these wires to the thumbtack holding the paper clip in place.

Buzz...............Are you there?
Buzz buzz............Yes
Long buzz............Help
Buzz, long buzz...Goodbye

Science explained

When you press the tapper, it completes the circuit. Electricity flows through the buzzer making it buzz. When you take your finger off the tapper, the circuit is broken and the buzzing stops.

Sending codes

Before the telephone was invented, a code called Morse was used to send messages. A set of short and long signals stood for each letter of the alphabet. Try making up your own code like the one above.

buzzer

This wire connects the buzzer to the battery.

This wire connects the buzzer to the switch.

This wire connects the battery to the switch.

4 Connect the loose wire from the buzzer to the battery. Use another wire to connect the thumbtack beneath the button to the battery. This is your tapper.

Buzz buzzzz

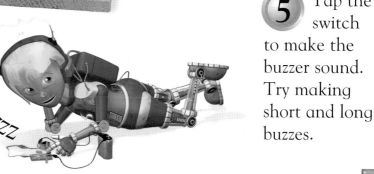

5 Tap the switch to make the buzzer sound. Try making short and long buzzes.

Electric fan

Electric motors can make things move. A washing machine, for example, has a powerful electric motor to move the laundry around. Why not set up a circuit with an electric motor that drives an electric fan to keep you cool?

Now make an electric fan
You will need: ★ a small electric motor ★ a battery ★ 2 small blocks of wood ★ 3 wires ★ a thick block of wood ★ a plastic propeller ★ a large, metal paper clip ★ 2 metal thumbtacks ★ glue ★ adhesive tape

1 Glue the thick block of wood to one of the small blocks.

large block of wood

small block of wood

propeller

spindle

motor

wires connected to motor

2 Ask an adult to help you glue the motor to the top of the thick block. Push the propeller onto the spindle of the motor.

3 Connect two wires to the motor. Ask an adult to help you make a paper clip switch with the other small block of wood, as shown on page 26.

High-speed train

This high-speed train is powered by electric motors. The electricity comes from power lines above the track.

4 Connect one wire from the motor to the battery and the other to the switch. Connect the battery and switch. To start the fan, turn the paper clip so it touches the thumbtack.

This wire connects the battery to the motor.

Wheee!

What happens if you swap the wires on the battery?

This wire connects the battery to the switch.

This wire connects the motor to the switch.

motor

spinning propeller

paper clip switch

 Be careful not to touch the fan when it is moving.

Electric tester

Electricity can flow through some materials. These are called conductors. It cannot flow through others. These are called insulators. Make this tester to find out which materials are conductors and which are insulators.

Now test some materials

You will need: ★ a battery ★ 3 wires ★ a bulb and bulb holder ★ different materials to test, such as a plastic ruler, a wooden pencil, and a metal spoon

wire attached to bulb holder

1 Connect two wires to the screws on the bulb holder.

wire connecting the battery to the bulb holder

2 Connect one wire to the end of the battery. Connect another wire to the other end of the battery.

Making electricity safe

The inside of an electric wire is metal, which is a conductor. The outside of a switch, wire, and plug are made from the insulator, plastic. Insulators protect us from the dangers of electricity and make it safe to use electric machines.

Science explained

When you test a conductor, it makes the circuit complete. Electricity flows through the conductor around the circuit and the bulb lights up. When you test an insulator, electricity cannot flow through it. The circuit is broken and the bulb does not light up.

This wire is connected to the battery.

This wire is connected to the bulb.

metal spoon

plastic spool of thread

metal paper clips

wooden pencil

plastic ruler

cord

3 Choose one of your objects to test, and connect the two loose wires to it. Does the bulb light up? Try testing the rest of the objects.

It's quiz time!

Now that you have completed the experiments, have fun testing your knowledge of electricity. Look back for help if you are unsure of any of the answers.

Let's go!

Can you find what doesn't belong?
Look at the lists of words below. Can you figure out which word in each line is unlike the others?

1 hair dryer   television   computer   bicycle

2 pencil   battery   bulb   wires

3 electric fan   burglar alarm   breakfast   code tapper

Can you choose the correct words?
Look at each sentence below. Choose which one of the three shaded words makes the sentence true.

1 A toaster needs (clothes) (electricity) (dinner) to work.

2 In a complete circuit, a (motor) (battery) (bulb) will light up.

3 Never experiment with household electricity. Instead, ask an adult to help you design a circuit with a (police officer) (teddy bear) (battery).

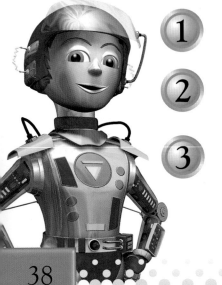

38

What's going on?
Can you answer the questions below?

1 How does this radio work when it is not plugged into the wall socket?

Buzz buzzzz

2 How does Pixel make the code tapper buzz?

3 How can you tell by looking at this circuit that the metal spoon conducts electricity?

Now check your answers.

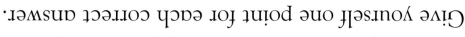

Give yourself one point for each correct answer.

Well done!
More than 3 points

Very good!!
More than 5 points

Brilliant!!!
More than 8 points

What's going on?
1 The radio has batteries in it, so it doesn't need to be plugged in.
2 When Pixel presses on the code tapper, she completes the electric circuit, making the buzzer work.
3 You can tell that the metal spoon conducts electricity because the light bulb is lit up.

Choose the correct words
1 Electricity
2 Bulb
3 Battery

What doesn't belong?
1 Bicycle – the others all need electricity to work.
2 Pencil – the others are all parts that make up an electrical circuit.
3 Breakfast – the others are all things you can make with an electrical circuit.

Forces and Movement

Parents' notes

This section will help your child to develop a basic understanding of forces, from describing different sorts of movement to relating movement to pushes and pulls. Read these notes and any on the relevant pages to help your child get the most out of the experiments.

Pages 44–45: On the move

This experiment encourages your child to recognize general types, directions, and speeds of movement. You might like to ask your child to think of some more movement words, for example, *twist*, *swerve*, or *slide*, and to act them out.

Pages 46–47: Starting force

Here your child is introduced to the concept of a starting force. There are different ways of creating a starting force, for example, hitting, pushing, or kicking a stationary object. After the balloon experiment, ask your child to choose another object and to find ways of moving it without using his or her hands.

Pages 48–49: Pushing things

Explain to your child that to make this a fair experiment, the box must be on the starting line each time he or she pushes it. You might like to discuss with your child the link between the weight of the box, the strength of the push needed to move it, and the distance it moves.

Pages 50–51: Pulling things

Make the hole in the cardboard for your child. This experiment shows the link between the weight of an object and the strength of the pull needed to move it. To help reinforce this idea, you might wish to supervise a tug-of-war game between your child and a friend.

Pages 52–53: Fast or slow?

Pushing and pulling forces can make things speed up, slow down, and stop. Your child will discover that by pushing or pulling the toy boats, he or she can control their speed. Your child might notice that changing the direction of the push or pull affects the speed, by speeding up or slowing down the movement.

Pages 54–55: Change direction

Here your child will learn how forces can affect the speed and direction of an object's motion. Encourage your child to try sucking air through the straw to see how this affects the table-tennis ball's direction. Your child will notice that the sucking force reverses the movement.

Pages 56–57: Push and pull

Encourage your child to experiment using other materials that bend and twist, such as clay or pastry dough, to make fun models. Ask your child to describe his or her actions, for example, stretching is pulling apart and squeezing is pushing together.

Pages 58–59: Friction

To make this test fair, the toy must be lined up with the ruler on a flat surface and be given the same strength push each time. Choose toys without wheels to avoid complications in understanding basic friction ideas.

Pages 60–61: Wind force

Discuss with your child how the push of the wind is a natural force that can move objects; for example, it can make a tree sway or laundry flap on the line. Encourage your child to test the kite in different weather conditions to see how well it flies.

Pages 62–63: Water force

Explain to your child that the push of moving water is another natural force that can make things move. If your child puts his or her hand first under a dripping faucet and then under a fully open faucet, he or she will be able to feel the powerful force that water can produce.

On the move

Look around. What can you see moving – birds flying, cars and bicycles speeding by, or people walking and running? Things move in different ways. They can speed up, slow down, or change direction. Moving makes the world an exciting place.

Now play this game
You will need: ★ a ruler ★ scissors ★ a felt-tip pen ★ some colored construction paper ★ a friend to play with

You can decorate your construction paper with stickers.

Moving words
- forward
- backward
- speed up
- slow down
- spin

1 Ask an adult to help you cut out five pieces of construction paper, each about 6 in (14 cm) long by 4 in (9 cm) wide.

2 Write each of these "moving" words on a different piece of construction paper. Lay all the cards face down.

spin

3 Pick a card and act out the word. Can your friend guess which movement you are acting out? If your friend guesses correctly, swap over.

spin

Super swings
If you go to a playground, you can see lots of people and things moving. It's great fun to swing in lots of different directions. You can make yourself swing fast or slow, too.

Science explained
Every time you or your friend go forward, backward, or turn around, you are moving. You know if something is moving because it changes its place or position. You can make your body move in different ways, in different directions, and at different speeds.

Starting force

How can you make a ball move? With a force, of course! A force is a knock that starts the ball moving. Without thinking about it, we use forces all the time. Kick a football – that's a force. Hit a tennis ball with a racket – that's another force.

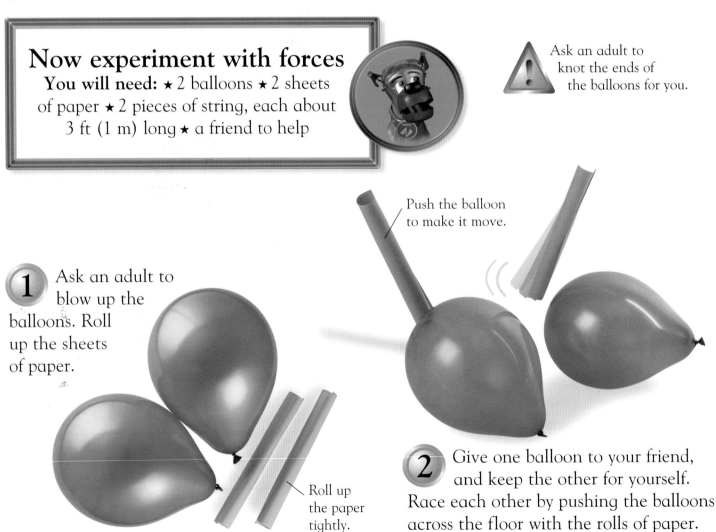

Now experiment with forces
You will need: ★ 2 balloons ★ 2 sheets of paper ★ 2 pieces of string, each about 3 ft (1 m) long ★ a friend to help

Ask an adult to knot the ends of the balloons for you.

Push the balloon to make it move.

1 Ask an adult to blow up the balloons. Roll up the sheets of paper.

Roll up the paper tightly.

2 Give one balloon to your friend, and keep the other for yourself. Race each other by pushing the balloons across the floor with the rolls of paper.

3 Now tie a piece of string to the end of each balloon.

4 Each hold onto a balloon string. Race your friend by pulling the balloons along the ground. Now try to kick or blow on the balloons. What happens?

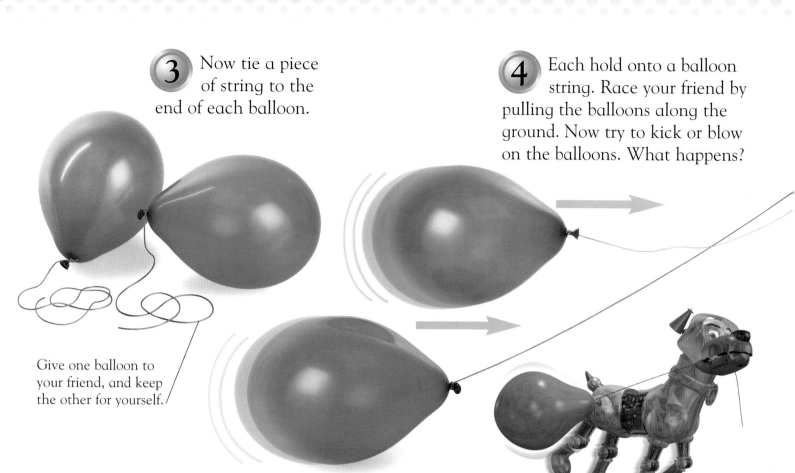

Give one balloon to your friend, and keep the other for yourself.

Science explained

A pull on a string, a push with a piece of rolled-up paper, a kick with your foot, and a puff of air from your mouth are all forces. You can use these forces to speed up a balloon. You can also use forces to stop a balloon from moving or to make it move in another direction.

Kicking force

A soccer player starts the ball moving by kicking it. A kick is a pushing force. If the player kicks the ball past the goalie and into the net, he scores a goal.

Pushing things

A push is a force. When you push on a door, it moves away from you. When you push a wheelbarrow, you can move it from place to place. If you push someone on a swing, he or she will go up in the air. The harder you push, the higher the person goes!

Pushing power

People use machines to push heavy things. Snowplows clear roads by pushing huge piles of snow to the sides.

Now try this pushing test
You will need: ★ masking tape
★ an empty toy box or cardboard box
★ lots of toys

1 Mark a starting line on the floor with the masking tape. Line up the empty toy box on the starting line. Give the box a push. How far does it go?

Fill the box with toys.

This is your starting line.

Science explained
An empty box is light. It's easy to move with a pushing force. When you add a few toys, the box is heavier and harder to push. It doesn't move as far as the empty box. The more toys you add, the heavier it becomes. If the box is too heavy, you can't move it at all!

2 Bring the box back to the starting line. Put a few toys into the box. Does the box move as easily? How far does it go? Now fill up the box with toys. Can you still push it?

Repeat the test, adding more toys each time.

Pulling things

Heave! A pull is a force that moves something toward you. A tractor pulls plows around the fields. In a tug-of-war, two teams pull on a rope. The team that tugs the hardest pulls the other team over the line.

Wheeee!

Now make a pull tester

You will need: ★ a piece of cardboard ★ a piece of string about 8 in (20 cm) long ★ a sharp pencil ★ a strong rubber band ★ 5 large books

1 Ask an adult to make a hole in one edge of the cardboard. Thread the string through the hole and the rubber band. Tie the string in a tight knot.

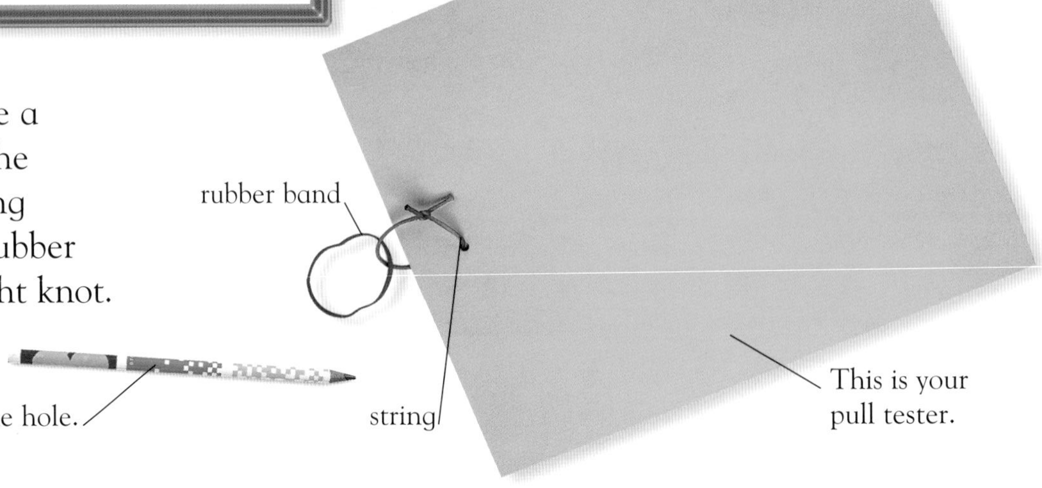

Use a pencil to make the hole.

rubber band

string

This is your pull tester.

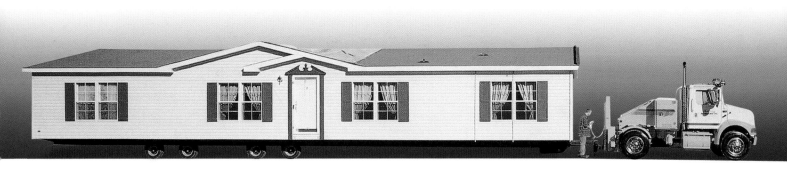

Powerful pulls

Some loads are too heavy for people to pull. Machines, such as tow trucks, are specially built to pull heavy loads. This giant tow truck is strong enough to pull a whole house!

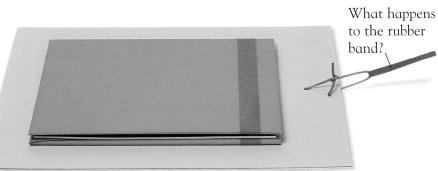

What happens to the rubber band?

Science explained

The rubber band only stretches a small amount with one book on the pull tester. A single book is light and only needs a weak pulling force to make it move. The more books you add, the harder it is to pull. The stronger the pulling force, the more the rubber band stretches.

2 Place one book on the cardboard. Pull the rubber band gently. How easy is it to pull the book?

What happens to the rubber band when more books are added to the pile?

3 Put two more books on the pile. What happens when you pull the rubber band? Now add the other books to the pile.

Be careful not to overstretch the rubber band, otherwise it will break.

Fast or slow?

It's fun to play on a merry-go-round. You push in one direction to speed it up, then pull in the opposite direction to slow it down. Experiment with pushing and pulling forces to make the boats change speed.

Now use pushes and pulls

You will need: ★ 2 toy boats
★ 2 pieces of string ★ a ruler
★ a large bowl of water

This experiment can be done in a bathtub of water, under adult supervision.

Push the boat with the ruler to start it moving.

Leave this string loose until step 3.

Pull the string to make the boat move and then speed up.

1 Put one boat in the water, and push it with a ruler. Give it another push to make it speed up. How can you slow down the boat?

2 Tie a piece of string to the back of one boat. Tie the other piece to the front and pull it. Pull it again to speed up the boat. How can you slow down the boat?

Speeding along

These people are whizzing across the water on boards. They each hold onto a rope attached to the speed boat. When the boat first pulls the rope, they start to move and then speed up.

Science explained

A push or pull makes the boat move. To speed it up, you push or pull again in the same direction. A push or pull in the opposite direction slows it down. When you tie two boats together and pull the front boat, the string between them tightens, pulling the second boat along.

3 Now tie the two boats together. Pull the string. What happens to both boats? How can you make the boats speed up or slow down?

Tie the boats together.

Pull this string to start the boats moving.

Change direction

Have you ever tried to walk a lively puppy on its leash when it pulls in different directions? It can be hard to walk in a straight line! Watch out – on a windy day, the wind's blowing force can also push you off course.

Grrr

Now blow a football
You will need: ★ a felt-tip pen ★ a large, shallow cardboard box or lid ★ 2 straws ★ a table-tennis ball ★ a friend to play with

You can color your football field green.

This is the starting point.

You and your friend each need a straw.

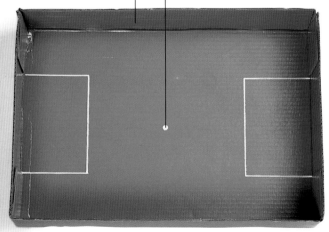

1 Use the pen to draw a rectangle at either end of the field. These are the goals. Draw a circle in the middle of the field.

2 Place the table-tennis ball on the starting point. Give each player a straw to blow through.

Ice hockey

This is a fast game. Hockey players zoom around the ice, changing direction by pushing on the ice with their skates. They hit a rubber block, called a puck, with ice-hockey sticks. This makes the puck change direction, so they can pass it to a teammate.

Science explained

The blowing forces push the ball to speed it up, slow it down, and change its direction. When something is moving in a straight line, a force, like a blow, can make it change direction. You and your friend are using blowing forces to make the ball move around the field.

3 Start the game. Try to score by blowing the ball into your friend's goal. Your friend tries to stop you scoring by blowing the ball off course, toward your goal.

Point the straw to make the ball move in the direction in which you want it to go.

Push and pull

Have you ever been pulled in two directions at once? You feel that you are being stretched. Have you ever

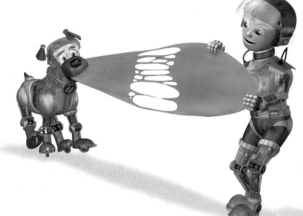

been pushed from both sides? Now you feel that you are being squashed. Forces can twist, bend, and roll things, too. Try using forces to make some shapes.

Now make a clay model
You will need: ★ a large piece of modeling clay or several small pieces of modeling clay

Use your fingers and thumbs to shape the clay.

1 Squeeze and squash a large lump of modeling clay in your hands.

Bend a shape between your thumb and fingers.

2 Stretch and bend two pieces of modeling clay.

3 Now roll some modeling clay into small pieces like these.

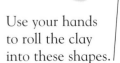

Use your hands to roll the clay into these shapes.

Making noodles

Noodle makers bend, twist, and pull the noodle mixture in their hands. When the noodles are the correct shape and size, they are ready to cook.

Twist the long shapes together.

Press firmly to make the shapes stick to your model.

This is a monster. What does your model look like?

4 Try twisting two of the pieces of rolled clay together.

Describe the force you use to make each new shape.

5 Put all the pieces together. Make some more shapes to add to your model. What forces are you using to make these other shapes?

57

Friction

Watch out! If you wear socks on a smooth floor, you'll slip and slide. But if you wear shoes on the same floor, you have a better grip. This is because of a special force, called friction, between your shoes and the floor. There is always friction when two things rub together, but different surfaces make different amounts of friction.

> **Now try this experiment**
> **You will need:** ★ a pencil ★ a sheet of paper ★ a ruler ★ a small toy ★ a tape measure ★ different surfaces, such as wood, grass, carpet, and vinyl

1 Draw a chart like this one. You will use the chart to record your findings.

	wood	grass	carpet	vinyl
rough or smooth				
distance				

You can decorate your chart.

This is your starting line.

2 Place the ruler on a wooden surface. Line up your toy just in front of the ruler.

Slippery slide

The pole in a fire station is made of smooth, shiny metal. This surface makes very little friction so the firefighters can slide down quickly. They need to get to the fire engines as fast as possible.

Science explained

The toy goes further on the smooth, hard wood or vinyl than it does on the rougher carpet or soft grass. Friction between the toy and the wood, grass, carpet, or vinyl slows down the toy. There is more friction on a rough or soft surface than there is on a smooth, hard surface.

Make sure the surface is flat.

To make the test fair, try to give the toy the same strength push when you repeat the test on other surfaces.

3 First, feel the wood. Is it rough or smooth? Fill in your chart. Now give the toy a push, and wait for it to stop.

4 Use the tape measure to see how far the toy went. Write down your results on the chart. Repeat the test on the other surfaces, and fill in the chart.

Wind force

On a windy day, hold onto your hat. The force of the wind could blow it off. The wind can blow leaves off trees, make flags flutter, and hold kites high in the air.

Now make a mini kite

You will need: ★ scissors ★ a ruler ★ a large sheet of paper ★ 3 straight straws, each 8 in (21 cm) long ★ a piece of string 6 ft (2 m) long ★ 2 ribbons or strips of paper ★ adhesive tape

1 Ask an adult to follow the measurements below to cut a diamond shape from the paper.

8 in (21 cm)

13 in (33 cm)

2 Squeeze one straw, and slide it inside another one. Tape them together.

Be careful when using scissors.

3 Trim these two straws to 13 in (33 cm) long. Tape the other straw 4 in (11 cm) from the top.

4 in (11 cm)

8 in (21 cm)

9 in (22 cm)

This is your crosspiece.

4 Tape the crosspiece to the four corners of the paper. Tie the string to the middle of the crosspiece.

Tie the string tightly to the crosspiece.

5 Tie the ribbons to the bottom of the crosspiece. Now you are ready to fly your kite outside in a gentle breeze. Run along holding your kite behind you.

If there is no wind, hold the string and run as fast as you can.

Wind power
This windsurfer is pushed across the sea by the wind's force. When the wind is stronger, its force pushes the board even faster over the choppy waves.

Science explained
The pushing force of the wind lifts your kite into the air. The pulling force from the string stops it from flying away. The blowing force of a breeze will keep your kite fluttering above your head. If the blowing force of the wind is too strong, it may break your kite.

Water force

Have you ever been pushed over by a wave in the sea? Moving water can push with a powerful force. We can use the force of water to turn a waterwheel. Water-wheels can work parts of machines. In the past, they were used to turn stones to grind flour.

Now make a waterwheel

You will need: ★ scissors ★ a piece of plastic-coated cardboard or plain cardboard ★ a ruler ★ modeling clay ★ an empty thread spool ★ a pencil

1 Ask an adult to help you cut out four squares of cardboard, each about 1 in (2.5 cm) by 1 in (2.5 cm).

2 Press four lumps of modeling clay around the spool. Push the pieces of cardboard firmly into the clay.

The pieces of cardboard are the paddles.

3 Thread the pencil through the spool. This is your waterwheel.

Make sure the spool spins freely around the pencil.

4 Hold onto one end of the pencil, and put one of the paddles under a running faucet. What happens?

Science explained

The moving water pushes on one piece of cardboard. This push makes the spool spin around, moving the next paddle into the path of the water. The water then pushes on this paddle. The wheel keeps spinning as the force of the water pushes on each paddle in turn.

Waterwheel

This waterwheel is powered by moving water. The force of the water pushes the waterwheel to keep it turning.

It's quiz time!

Now that you have completed the experiments, have fun testing your knowledge of forces. Look back for help if you are unsure of any of the answers.

Let's go!

 Can you find what doesn't belong?
Look at the lists of words below. Can you figure out which word in each line is unlike the others?

1 blow   pull   balloon   kick

2 read   roll   squeeze   squash

3 forward   spin   backward   toy

How's it going?

Can you choose the correct words?
Look at each sentence below. Choose which one of the three shaded words makes the sentence true.

1 When you run you are
(eating)   (moving)   (sleeping).

2 A kite can stay in the sky because of the force of the
(snow)   (rain)   (wind).

3 To make a table-tennis ball change direction, you can (blow)   (speak)   (drink) through a straw.

64

What's going on?
Can you answer the questions below?

1 What force is making this wheel turn around?

2 Newton wants to go in a different direction from Pixel. How is he trying to make her change direction?

Grrr

Wheeee!

3 What type of force is Chip using to move Newton?

Now check your answers.

Give yourself one point for each correct answer.

Well done!
More than 3 points

Very good!!
More than 5 points

Brilliant!!!
More than 8 points

What doesn't belong!
1 Balloon – the other words all describe types of forces.
2 Read – the other words are all pushing forces.
3 Toy – the other words all describe types of movement.

Choose the correct words
1 Moving
2 Wind
3 Blow

What's going on?
1 The pushing force of the water is turning the wheel around.
2 Newton is pulling in a different direction from Pixel.
3 Chip is using a pulling force to move Newton.

65

Light and Color

Parents' notes

This section will help to develop your child's understanding of light and color and to relate it to his or her everyday experiences. Read these notes and any on the relevant pages to help your child get the most out of the experiments.

Pages 70–71: Sunlight

This activity enables your child to see the most important natural source of light – sunlight – clearly and safely. Make sure he or she does this experiment on a sunny day. You will need to help your child make the hole in the card. Explain why he or she should never look directly at the Sun.

Pages 72–73: In the dark

Make sure that the cubbyhole is safe, and help your child to move around safely with the blindfold on. Discuss the other senses he or she is relying on when blindfolded. Ask your child to describe and compare the different stages of darkness he or she experiences.

Pages 74–75: Lamps and lights

This experiment will help your child to observe how the brightness and quality of the light from different sources varies. Make sure he or she is aware of the dangers of candles and knows only to use matches under adult supervision.

Pages 76–77: Light and shade

This activity helps your child to understand that shadows are formed when a solid object blocks the passage of light. Encourage him or her to move the puppets back and forth. This will demonstrate how the shape and size of the shadow is affected by the distance of the object from the light source. Your child could also make animal shadows with his or her hands.

Pages 78–79: Bright and dim

This experiment encourages your child to investigate how the brightness of a patch of light decreases as its distance from the source increases. He or she should observe how the patch spreads to light up a larger area, but with less brightness, as the distance gets greater. Ask your child to describe how the light changes.

Pages 80–81: Bouncing light

Light rays bounce off smooth, shiny surfaces, such as mirrors, glass, and water. The game featured on this page emphasizes this point and also demonstrates that light can be controlled and redirected to where your child wants it.

Pages 82–83: Rainbow colors

Explain to your child that sunlight is actually a mixture of the colors of the rainbow. This mixture makes white light. However, when there is sunshine and rain, the raindrops split the mixture up into its basic colors and a rainbow forms in the sky. We normally count seven separate colors in the rainbow: red, orange, yellow, green, blue, indigo, and violet.

Pages 84–85: Mixing colors

Here your child will learn that he or she can create many different colors, by mixing the three primary colors, red, yellow, and blue. Ensure the brush is cleaned between mixing.

Pages 86–87: Colored light

Explain to your child that an object only looks a particular color because it reflects colored light. The glasses show how, for example, looking through red cellophane only lets red light through. A green object appears dark viewed through red glasses. This is because the red cellophane blocks the green light that the green object reflects.

Pages 88–89: Bright colors

When your child has completed this experiment, discuss why some colors show up better than others. Bright colors from the middle of the rainbow, such as yellow and orange, reflect the most light and so show up the best. Dull or dark colors reflect less light and so do not show up as well. The silvery pieces of glitter reflect light like tiny mirrors, so they shine brightly in the beam of the flashlight. Encourage your child to think about when and why it is important to wear brightly colored clothes.

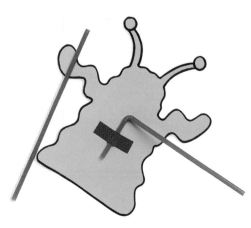

Sunlight

Your eyes need light to see. Light comes from many sources, such as electric lights. The most important light source is the Sun. Light travels from the Sun in straight lines, called rays, to Earth.

Now catch some sunlight
You will need: ★ 2 pieces of cardboard ★ a sharp pencil

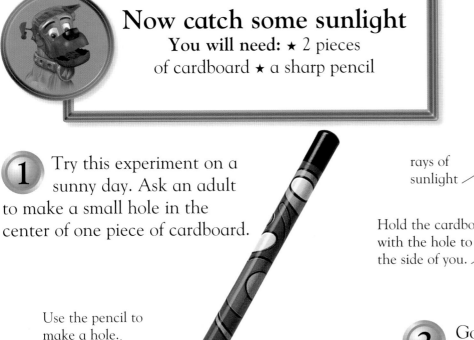

rays of sunlight

Hold the cardboard with the hole to the side of you.

1 Try this experiment on a sunny day. Ask an adult to make a small hole in the center of one piece of cardboard.

Use the pencil to make a hole.

2 Go outside and stand with your back to the Sun. Hold the cardboard with the hole so that it faces the Sun. Hold the other piece of cardboard about 10 in (25 cm) below it.

Move the bottom piece of cardboard around until you can see a circle of light.

Great ball of fire

The Sun is the nearest star to planet Earth. It is a huge ball of burning gas far out in space. The Sun burns very brightly and gives out light and heat. We need light and heat for life on this planet.

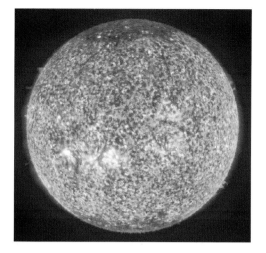

Science explained

Light rays from the Sun travel straight through the hole in the cardboard and spread out on the cardboard below. These light rays make up a complete picture of the Sun, called an image. If you move the pieces of cardboard further apart, the picture of the Sun gets bigger.

The bright circle of light that you see is a picture of the Sun.

3 Now try moving the cardboard pieces further apart, like Pixel is doing. How does the picture of the Sun change?

In the dark

At night, when the Sun goes down, it gets dark outside, and it's hard to see. It's dark in the movie theater before the film starts, and under the bedclothes at night. Darkness is where there is no light.

Now make it dark

You will need: ★ sunglasses ★ a thick scarf or piece of material ★ 2 chairs ★ a thick blanket ★ a book

2 Next, throw a blanket over the backs of two chairs to make a dark cubbyhole. Crawl inside and pull the blanket over the chairs.

Can you read the book with sunglasses on?

1 Draw the curtains and switch off any lights. Put on the sunglasses. Try reading the book.

Science explained

Your eyes can still see in dim light with sunglasses on. It's more difficult to see in the cubbyhole. You can't see with a thick blindfold on – it blocks out all the light. In total darkness, your senses of touch and hearing help you to find your way.

Dark places

Deep caves and thick forests are always dark, even in the daytime, because light from the Sun cannot reach inside them.

Can you read the book in your cubbyhole?

Try to block out all the light in your cubbyhole.

3 Ask an adult to tie a scarf over your eyes. With his or her help, carefully move around. Is it easier to move around if you feel objects and listen for sounds?

Try to find things with your blindfold on.

Lamps and lights

When darkness falls at night, we use many different things to give us light. In the past, candle flames and fires helped people to see in the dark. Today, there are lots of light sources, from overhead lights to flashlights. All of these light sources give out light in different ways.

Now test some light sources
You will need: ★ a sheet of paper ★ a ruler ★ colored pencils ★ different light sources, such as a candle, flashlight, table lamp, spotlight, and overhead light

1 Draw a chart like this one. List the different light sources and the different kinds of light they make.

Light source	Spotlight	Flashlight	Overhead light	Candle	Table lamp
Bright light					
Dim light					
Steady light					
Flickering light					
Beam of light					
Lights up whole room					
Lights up small area					

Draw pictures of your light sources, like the ones shown here.

2 Draw the curtains and switch off any lights to make the room dark. Now switch on the light sources, one at a time.

table lamp

Always ask an adult to light candles for you. Never play with matches or candles.

candle

overhead light

spotlight

flashlight

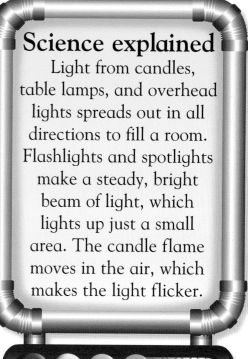

Miner's light
A miner has an electric light on his helmet. It sends out a bright beam that lights up the tunnel when he's working deep underground.

Science explained
Light from candles, table lamps, and overhead lights spreads out in all directions to fill a room. Flashlights and spotlights make a steady, bright beam of light, which lights up just a small area. The candle flame moves in the air, which makes the light flicker.

3 Look at the types of light that each light source gives out. Record what you can see on your chart by checking the boxes, like Pixel and Newton are doing.

You may have more than one check for each light source.

Light and shade

Do you ever try to catch your own shadow when you're outside on a bright, sunny day? Shadows are made when light falls on a solid object, such as your body. Your body blocks the light, and this makes a dark area of shade.

Now make some shadows

You will need: ★ a felt-tip pen ★ scissors ★ pieces of cardboard ★ adhesive tape ★ 2 chairs ★ bendy straws ★ a spotlight ★ a long piece of string ★ clothespins ★ a white sheet

1 Draw some space alien shapes on the cardboard, and cut them out.

2 Use the adhesive tape to stick a straw to each alien.

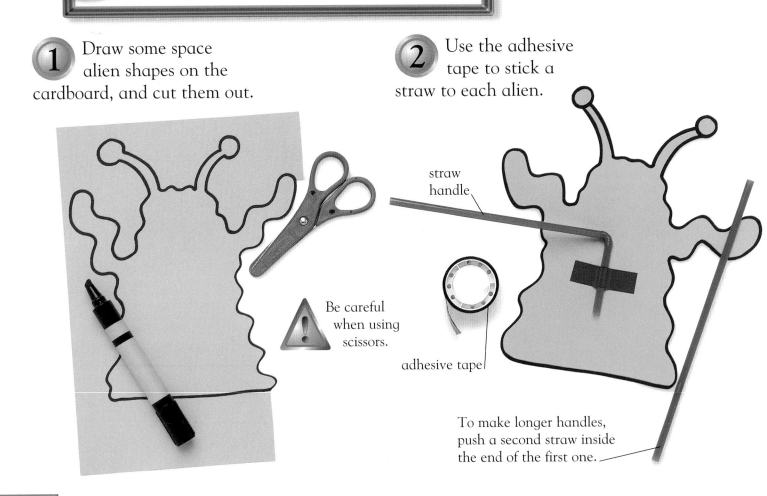

straw handle

Be careful when using scissors.

adhesive tape

To make longer handles, push a second straw inside the end of the first one.

Changing shadows

In the morning, when the Sun rises, shadows are long. At midday, when the Sun is high overhead, shadows are much shorter.

Your audience watches the show from the other side of the sheet.

puppet's shadow

The light shines through the white sheet.

What happens if you move the puppets closer to the light?

3 Tie the string between two chairs. Hang the sheet on the string. Ask an adult to help you put the light safely behind the sheet.

4 Hold the puppets between the lamp and the sheet, like Pixel and Newton are doing. The puppets will cast shadows on the sheet. What shapes are the shadows?

Bright and dim

When you are traveling on dark roads at night, the headlights of cars a long way away look dim. But as they get closer, the lights get brighter and brighter, until they dazzle your eyes. The closer you get to a light, the brighter it looks.

Now shine a light

You will need: ★ a flashlight ★ a large sheet of paper ★ sticky tack ★ a felt-tip pen ★ a friend to help

2 Draw the curtains and switch off any lights. Switch on the flashlight, and hold it about 6 in (15 cm) away from the paper. How bright is the patch of light?

1 Attach a large sheet of paper to the wall with some sticky tack.

The flashlight forms a patch of light, with a bright spot in the middle.

Science explained

A flashlight shines a bright patch of light on the wall when it is held near the wall. As you move the flashlight away from the wall, the light spreads out from the light source. This makes the light patch bigger, but dimmer.

Warning light

At night, lighthouses on rocky coasts flash beams of light as warnings to passing ships. Sailors know that the brighter the light looks, the closer they are to danger.

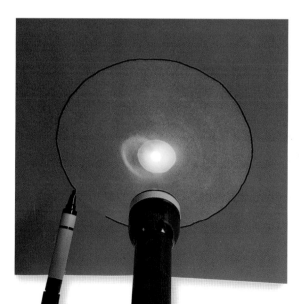

Hold the flashlight still.

3 Ask your friend to draw around the whole patch of light on the paper with a felt-tip pen.

Shine the flashlight on the same spot.

4 Now move about 7 ft (2 m) away from the wall, and shine the flashlight on the paper, like Chip is doing. Ask your friend to draw around the light patch now. How has it changed?

Bouncing light

On a sunny day, your eyes can be dazzled by sunlight bouncing, or reflecting, off of a shiny metal car or water in a swimming pool. Any smooth, shiny surface can reflect bright light. Mirrors reflect light best of all.

Now bounce a light

You will need: ★ a bright flashlight ★ a box ★ a watch with a second hand ★ a small mirror ★ 5 sheets of paper ★ a felt-tip pen ★ sticky tack ★ a bowl ★ a friend to help

1 On each sheet of paper, draw around the bowl. Number the sheets of paper from 1 to 5 to make targets.

2 Use sticky tack to attach the targets to a wall. Stand the flashlight up on a box in the middle of the room. Turn on the flashlight.

The box raises the flashlight off the ground.

Ball of mirrors

A large ball covered in tiny mirrors, like this one, is often hung from the ceiling in a disco. It is used to bounce, or reflect, colored lights all around the room. As the ball spins, the walls and ceiling are covered in moving patches of light.

Science explained

Light travels in straight lines. When the light from the flashlight hits the mirror, it bounces off, or is reflected, in a new direction. By moving the mirror, you can change the direction of the reflected light and make it move around the room.

number target

3 Hold the mirror near the flashlight. Tilt the mirror to bounce the light onto one of the targets.

You may need to change the position of the mirror to hit the target.

4 Now ask your friend to call out numbers from 1 to 5. By moving the mirror, how many targets can you hit in 30 seconds?

Rainbow colors

Have you ever seen a rainbow? Rainbows appear when there is sunshine and rain at the same time. Even though sunlight looks white, it's really made up of different colors. As the sunlight passes through the raindrops, it splits into its rainbow colors.

Now make a rainbow
You will need: ★ a shallow dish ★ a bright flashlight ★ a pitcher of water ★ a mirror with plastic edge ★ a piece of white cardboard ★ a friend to help

1 Place the dish on a table. Fill it half full with water from the pitcher.

Be careful not to spill the water.

2 Stand the mirror in the water so that it is at an angle to the bottom of the dish. Ask a friend to shine the flashlight toward the bottom of the mirror.

The light beam must shine through the water and hit the bottom of the mirror.

Hold the flashlight steady.

Over the rainbow

When the Sun is shining, you can often see a rainbow over a waterfall. The spray from the falling water works just like rain, splitting sunlight into the seven different colors of the rainbow.

Science explained

Light from a flashlight is made up of a mixture of colors. When you shine the light through water onto the mirror, the colors split up. You can see the seven rainbow colors on the cardboard: red, orange, yellow, green, blue, indigo, and violet.

3 Ask your friend to hold the cardboard as well as the flashlight. Tilt the mirror so that you can see the light on the cardboard. What else can you see?

Look for the seven colors of the rainbow.

Mixing colors

Look closely at the plants in a garden – how many different colors can you see? Your eyes can see thousands of different colors. You can make lots of these colors by mixing together just three different colors of paint.

Now mix some colors

You will need: ★ a ruler ★ red, yellow, and blue paints ★ a paintbrush ★ a large cup of water ★ a plate ★ a sheet of white paper ★ a felt-tip pen

Clean your brush in the water after using each color.

This is your color wheel.

1 Place the plate on the paper and draw around the plate. Use a ruler to divide the circle into six parts.

2 Paint one part of the wheel red, one yellow, and one blue. Leave gaps in between each one.

Paint the whole of each part in one color.

Artist's paints

Artists use their knowledge of the color wheel to mix colors on a palette. With just a few basic colored paints, they can make all the colors they need for their paintings.

Science explained

You can make different colors and shades by mixing red, yellow, and blue paints in different amounts. Mixing red and yellow paint makes the color orange, mixing red and blue makes purple, and mixing blue and yellow makes green.

Mix red and blue paint together to make a new color for this part.

What color do you get when you mix red and yellow?

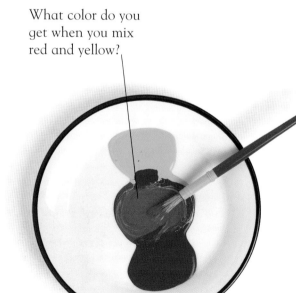

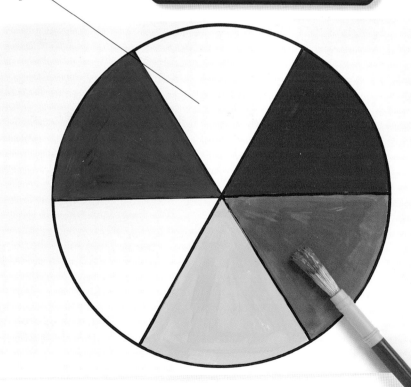

3 Next, mix some red and yellow paint together on the plate. Use it to paint the part of your wheel between red and yellow.

4 Now mix red and blue paint. Fill in the part between red and blue. Mix blue and yellow paint. Fill in the part between blue and yellow. What colors have you made?

Colored light

Light can pass straight through clear, or transparent, materials, such as a glass window. If you shine light through colored glass or plastic, it changes color. Try looking at the world through differently colored glasses.

Now make colored glasses

You will need: ★ a piece of cardboard ★ scissors ★ a ruler ★ a felt-tip pen ★ red, yellow, blue, and green cellophane ★ adhesive tape ★ red, yellow, blue, and green objects

eyehole

arm

Draw the frame with the felt-tip pen.

2 Ask an adult to help you cut out the glasses. Tape two squares of red cellophane over the eyeholes. Put on your glasses. How does the world look?

1 Draw a simple glasses frame on the cardboard. Ask an adult to make sure that the eyeholes match the distance between your eyes and that the arms are long enough to sit on your ears.

Make the frames wide enough for the adhesive tape.

Cut out small squares of cellophane to fit over the eyeholes.

Be careful when using scissors.

Sort your objects into groups of the same color.

3 Sort your objects into groups by color. Now put on your glasses and look at each group in turn. Do the colors of the objects change or do they stay the same as when you looked at them without the glasses on?

4 Now try putting yellow, green, or blue cellophane in the glasses, instead of red. What happens when you look at the groups of objects now?

Green for go!

The red, amber, and green lights in traffic lights are made of bright, white lightbulbs behind see-through colored plastic covers. A red light warns drivers of danger and tells them to stop. A green light means drivers can go if it is safe.

Science explained

When you look at differently colored objects through red glasses, some of them change color. Red objects are still red, but other objects look dark. This is because the red cellophane lets only red light through. It blocks out the other colors of the rainbow.

Bright colors

Police officers wear brightly colored jackets when they are directing traffic. This helps drivers to see them clearly, especially when it is dark. Which do you think are the best colors to wear for safety at night?

Now test different colors
You will need: ★ a bright flashlight ★ scissors ★ a sheet of black paper ★ felt-tip pens ★ white stickers ★ silver glitter ★ nontoxic glue ★ sticky tack

Make four folds in the paper strip.

Be careful when using scissors.

3 Next, color two stickers in bright colors and two more in dark colors. Glue some glitter on the fifth sticker.

Dab some glue on a sticker and sprinkle the glitter on top.

1 Fold over one end of a sheet of black paper. Next, fold the paper the other way. Do the same again, until all the paper folds into a zigzag.

2 Draw the outline of a person that fills the paper. Carefully, cut out the shape to make a paper chain of five people.

Glow in the dark

For safety, road workers and emergency teams wear bright fluorescent jackets that glow in the dark. These colors shine brightly in the light from passing traffic.

Science explained

Bright colors, such as yellow and orange, show up best in the dark because they reflect more light. Dark colors, such as brown and purple, reflect less light. They do not show up as well. The silver glitter reflects light, so it shines brightly in the light.

colored sticker

4 Stick one colored sticker onto each of the people in your paper chain. Use sticky tack to stick the paper chain onto a wall.

Use two brightly colored felt-tip pens and two dark ones.

5 Draw the curtains and turn out the light. Which color is hardest to see in the dark? Now switch on the flashlight, and shine the light on the people one at a time.

Which color shows up best in the light?

It's quiz time!

Now that you have completed the experiments, have fun testing your knowledge of light and color. Look back for help if you are unsure of any of the answers.

Let's go!

Can you find what doesn't belong?
Look at the lists of words below. Can you figure out which word in each line is unlike the others?

1   flashlight   sunglasses   candle   lamp

2   blue   paintbrush   red   yellow

3   cave   mug   cubbeyhole   movie theater

How's it going?

Can you choose the correct words?
Look at each sentence below. Choose which one of the three shaded words makes the sentence true.

1   When you're outside, light comes from the
(clouds)   (Sun)   (trees) .

2   A rainbow appears in the sky when there is sunshine and (clouds)   (wind)   (rain) at the same time.

3   A light from a candle makes a
(flickering)   (flashing)   (pink) light.

What's going on?

Can you answer the questions below?

1 Why does Newton wear such a bright jacket at nighttime?

2 Pixel and Newton are giving a shadow-puppet show. How are they making the shadows?

3 Which two colors are mixed to make orange on a color wheel?

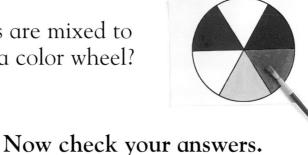

Now check your answers.

Give yourself one point for each correct answer.

 Well done! More than 3 points

 **Very good!** More than 5 points

 **Brilliant!!!** More than 8 points

What doesn't belong!
1 Sunglasses – the others are all sources of light.
2 Paintbrush – the others are all colors.
3 Mug – the others are all places that are dark, even during the day.

Choose the correct words
1 Sun
2 Rain
3 Flickering

What's going on?
1 Newton's bright jacket is easy for drivers to see in the dark – it helps keep him safe.
2 The puppets are in front of the light, and their shadows fall on the screen. People on the other side of the screen can see the shadows.
3 The colors red and yellow are mixed to make orange on a color wheel.

Sound and Music

Parents' notes

This section will help your child to become aware of the different sounds that he or she hears, and to develop an understanding of the sources of sounds. Read these notes and any on the relevant pages to help your child get the most out of the experiments.

Pages 96–97: Hearing sounds

This experiment encourages your child to focus on the everyday sounds that he or she can hear. Discussing hearing as one of the five senses will also help you to introduce the other senses: sight, touch, smell, and taste.

Pages 98–99: Making sounds

Sounds are created by fast shaking movements, called vibrations, that travel invisibly through the air. Explain to your child that when you speak, two vocal cords in your windpipe vibrate as air passes between them, creating sound waves. Encourage your child to think of different ways of making sounds.

Pages 100–101: Tracking sounds

You use both ears to detect where sounds come from. Discuss with your child how locating a sound helps you recognize hazards, such as a speeding fire engine. Explain that to make the experiment on this page fair, each tap should be the same strength. It is important to explain why it is dangerous to insert things into ears.

Pages 102–103: Faraway sounds

As sound waves travel away from their source they spread out, becoming fainter. A megaphone channels sound waves in one direction, stopping them from spreading out too much. The shell-like shape of the outer ear helps to collect and channel sound waves.

Pages 104–105: Striking sounds

Different materials make different sounds. When your child hits a metal object, it makes a clear, ringing sound. A soft fabric object makes a dull sound. This is because the metal object vibrates more quickly and for a longer time.

Pages 106–107: Loud and soft

On these pages, your child will learn that the loudness of the sound depends on how hard the drum is beaten. Encourage your child to make loud and soft sounds on the drum using different beaters.

Pages 108–109: High and low

This experiment demonstrates how the pitch of a sound can be changed by making an object vibrate at different speeds. Short, thin elastic bands vibrate more quickly than long, thick ones and so produce higher notes.

Pages 110–111: Bouncing sound

This experiment will show your child how echoes are made. Sounds reflect off hard surfaces and bounce back to the ears as echoes. Encourage your child to compare the results of this experiment with those achieved by speaking into objects made of soft fabrics.

Pages 112–113: Sound travels

For safety reasons, an adult needs to make the hole in the end of each paper cup. This experiment demonstrates to your child that sound waves can travel through a solid object, such as string, as well as through air. Encourage your child to see what happens when the telephone string is held loosely.

Pages 114–115: Block out sounds

Soft materials, such as towels, cotton balls, and bubble wrap are all good for soundproofing. Encourage your child to experiment with different materials to see which have the best soundproofing qualities. He or she might like to think of places that need to be soundproof, for example, a radio studio.

Hearing sounds

Listen carefully! What can you hear? People talking, dogs barking, phones ringing – there are lots of different sounds. Some are nice to listen to, like music on the radio. Others are just noise, like a flying plane.

Now make a sound chart
You will need: ★ a sheet of paper ★ 20 buttons, counters, or coins ★ colored pencils ★ a ruler ★ a watch or clock with a second hand

1 Draw a chart like this one with pictures to show different sorts of everyday sounds.

At the top of each column, draw a picture like this, or choose your own.

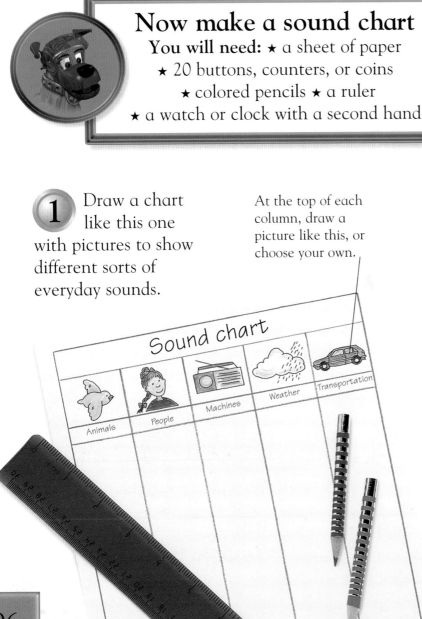

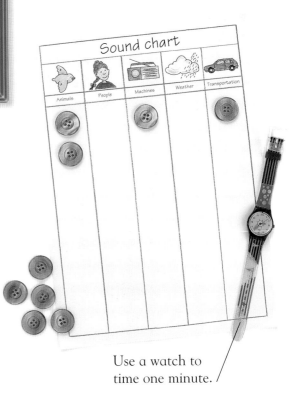

Use a watch to time one minute.

2 For one minute, listen carefully for the different types of sounds you can hear. Each time you hear a new sound, place a button in one of the columns on your chart.

City and countryside sounds

In the busy city streets, you can hear lots of loud noises, such as traffic rumbling and car horns honking. Out in the countryside, the sounds are quieter and more peaceful. You can hear birds singing, cows mooing, and the leaves on the trees rustling.

Sound chart

Animals	People	Machines	Weather	Transportation

Repeat the test at nighttime. Do you get the same results?

3 At the end of the minute, count the buttons in each column. Which type of sound did you hear the most?

Science explained

Hearing is one of your five senses. You hear sounds with your ears. The outsides of your ears are cup-shaped, which helps them to collect different sounds from all around you. Your ears send messages to your brain to tell you what sounds you are hearing.

Making sounds

If you twang an rubber band, it moves back and forth very quickly, making a sound. This shaking movement is called a vibration. Sound vibrations are often too fast to see, but you can sometimes feel them.

Now make different sounds
You will need: ★ 2 plastic cups ★ a plastic ruler ★ a plastic bucket or bowl ★ 2 spoons ★ marbles, dry lentils, or rice ★ adhesive tape ★ a table

1 Tape a ruler onto the edge of a table. Press down on the free end, then let go.

First tap the bucket gently, and then tap it harder.

Can you make twanging sounds with the ruler?

Make sure the ruler is firmly taped to the table.

2 Turn a plastic bucket upside down. Can you tap or bang a rhythm on the bottom of the bucket with the spoons?

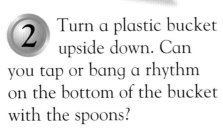

98

Science explained

When you twang, bang, and rattle different things, they move and shake and make sounds. These shaking movements or vibrations travel through the air as waves of sound, just like ripples moving through water. You hear sounds when these sound waves enter your ears.

Making music

You can make sounds by blowing air down a musical instrument called a recorder. The shaking movement of the air inside the recorder makes a sound. You can change the sound by covering up the holes on the recorder.

adhesive tape

Move the cups from side to side.

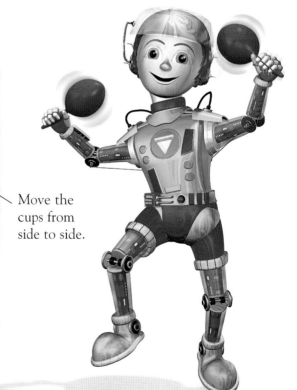

3 Tape together two cups filled with some marbles. What different sounds can you make by rattling the marbles in your shaker?

Tracking sounds

Put your hand over one of your ears. Can you still hear sounds with the other ear? If it's possible to hear with just one ear, why do you have two? The answer is that having two ears helps you to figure out where a sound is coming from.

Now test your ears
You will need: ★ 3 ft (1 m) of flexible plastic tubing or hose pipe ★ 3 adhesive labels ★ a pen ★ a pencil ★ a friend to help

1 Write the numbers 1 to 3 on the adhesive labels.

1

2

3

2 Stick the labels onto the tubing – space them out evenly.

3

1

numbered label

2

Warning bells

Knowing where a sound is coming from can be important. When a fire engine rushes along with its sirens blaring, you need to know where it is. The noise warns you to get out of the way!

Science explained
It is easy to tell which number label your friend taps when you listen with both ears. If the tap is closer to one ear than the other, the sound is louder on that side. If you listen with one ear, it is harder to work out where the sound comes from.

3 Gently hold the ends of the tubing to the outsides of your ears. Close your eyes. Ask your friend to tap one of the labels on the tube with a pencil. Can you tell which label your friend is tapping?

4 Now take the tubing away from one ear, and try the test again, like Pixel and Newton are doing. Can you tell where your friend is tapping?

Bend the tubing
into a curve.

2

Faraway sounds

It can be difficult to hear a sound when you are far away from it. If your friends tried to talk to you from the far side of the playground, you would have trouble hearing what they were saying – even if they shouted! This is because a sound gets quieter as it travels away from its starting point.

Now use a megaphone

You will need: ★ a large, thick sheet of paper ★ adhesive tape ★ scissors ★ a friend to help

1 Roll a large sheet of paper into the shape of a cone.

wide end

narrow end

Be careful when using scissors.

Tape the cone securely.

2 Stick the cone together with tape. Trim the wide end of the cone with scissors.

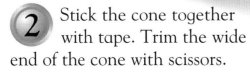

Listening in a crowd

It can be hard to hear at the back of a crowd. At a concert, performers usually sing into microphones, which are connected to speakers and a machine that increases, or amplifies, the sound. This helps their voices travel to the back of the audience so that everyone can hear.

3 Go outside and stand in front of your friend. Ask him or her to talk. Then ask him or her to speak through the megaphone.

Hello

Hello

H e l l o

Does your friend's voice sound louder than usual?

4 Now walk away from your friend, like Pixel is doing. How far do you have to go before you can no longer hear your friend?

Striking sounds

Try tapping gently on things made of different materials – a table, the fridge, the sofa. What kinds of sounds do they make? Now find out why different materials make different sounds.

Percussion band

This exciting percussion band called *Stomp* uses everyday things to make amazing musical sounds. The musicians bang on metal garbage cans for drums and tap out rhythms on plastic barrels.

Now play the chimes

You will need: ★ scissors ★ a ball of string ★ a coat hanger ★ adhesive tape ★ a metal spoon ★ objects made of wood, pottery, metal, fabric, and plastic

Tie the string tightly.

Be careful when using scissors.

1 Tie or tape a piece of string to each of your objects.

2 Tie or tape the other end of each string to a coat hanger. Hang the objects in a row, so that they can swing freely. These are your chimes.

3 Hang up the coat hanger. Tap each chime in turn with a metal spoon. How does each chime sound?

Which material makes the loudest sound when you tap it?

Science explained

When you tap the hanging object, it shakes, or vibrates, and makes a sound. The chimes made of hard materials, such as metal, make loud, clear ringing sounds. Materials such as wood make soft, duller sounds. Soft objects made of fabric make hardly any sound at all.

Loud and soft

Some sounds, like a whisper, are soft and quiet. Others, like a shout or the noise of stamping feet, are loud. Make this drum to see how you can make both loud and soft sounds.

Now bang a drum

You will need: ★ a sheet of thin plastic ★ a plastic bucket or bowl ★ adhesive tape ★ scissors ★ 2 pencils ★ rubber bands ★ a paintbrush ★ a wooden spoon

1 Stretch the plastic over the top of the bucket. Hold the plastic in place with a rubber band, and tape it to the bucket.

2 Wrap several rubber bands around the end of each pencil to make your drumsticks.

Stretch the plastic tightly to make your drum.

Be careful when using scissors.

Use the rubber bands to cover the pencil ends.

Marching band

Drummers are important members of a marching band. They keep time by banging a regular beat on the drums for the other musicians to follow. In this way, everyone plays the music at the same speed and to the same rhythm.

Aargh!

3 Bang the drum with your drumsticks. Can you make soft and loud sounds?

Can you tap a rhythm in time to some music?

wooden spoon

paintbrush

4 Now try experimenting with different drum sticks. Which drumsticks make the softest and loudest sounds?

Science explained

The strength you use to bang your drum affects the loudness of the sound. If you tap gently on the drum, it makes soft sounds. If you bang hard, the drum makes loud sounds. The loudness of the sound also depends on the hardness of the material that your drumstick is made of.

High and low

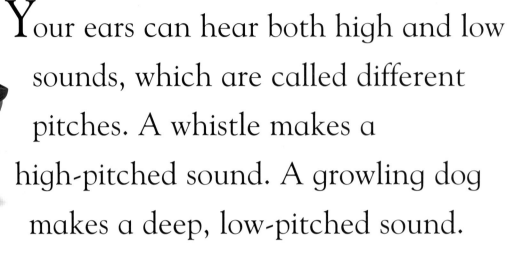

Grrrrr

Your ears can hear both high and low sounds, which are called different pitches. A whistle makes a high-pitched sound. A growling dog makes a deep, low-pitched sound.

In music, different pitched sounds are called notes.

Now play a box guitar

You will need: ★ a strong, plastic or metal box without a lid ★ thick and thin rubber bands ★ a pencil

1 Stretch several rubber bands over the box to make your box guitar.

The rubber bands are the strings on your guitar.

thick rubber band

thin rubber band

2 Now pluck each of the strings one by one. Which strings make the highest notes? Which make the lowest notes?

Plucking strings

Banjo players and guitarists play tunes by plucking the banjo and guitar strings. Thin or short strings make the highest notes. To play higher notes, the musicians shorten the strings by pressing them down on the neck of the banjo or guitar.

Your pencil needs to fit across the box.

4 Slide the pencil up and down the guitar as you pluck the bands. How do the notes change? Try playing a tune to a friend.

Do the notes sound different with the pencil?

3 Push a pencil under the strings to stretch the rubber bands. Pluck the strings again.

Ping

Bouncing sound

Have you ever shouted your name near a cliff? It sounds as if someone is shouting back at you. The sound you hear is called an echo. Inside a cave, you may hear several echoes, one after the other, which can sound spooky!

Now make an echo
You will need: ★ a clean, plastic cup ★ a small, clean, plastic bucket ★ a clean, plastic wastepaper basket or a large, plastic bucket

2 Now bring the bucket up to your mouth as you count "One, two, three ...." Does the sound of your voice change?

One, two, three ...

plastic cup

1 Start counting in a loud voice, "One, two, three ...." Bring the cup up to your mouth as you count. Does the sound of your voice change?

One, two, three ...

plastic bucket

Fun echoes

You can also hear echoes inside a tunnel with hard walls. At an amusement park, the passengers on an exciting roller-coaster ride can hear echoes of their screams as they whizz through a tunnel.

One, two, three ...

plastic wastepaper basket

3 Finally, repeat the numbers into the wastepaper basket. Which container makes the loudest echoes?

What happens to your voice when you talk into the wastepaper basket?

Sound travels

Press your ear against a wall. Can you hear or feel anything? You can hear and feel sound vibrations because sound waves can travel through different materials, as well as the air, before they reach your ears.

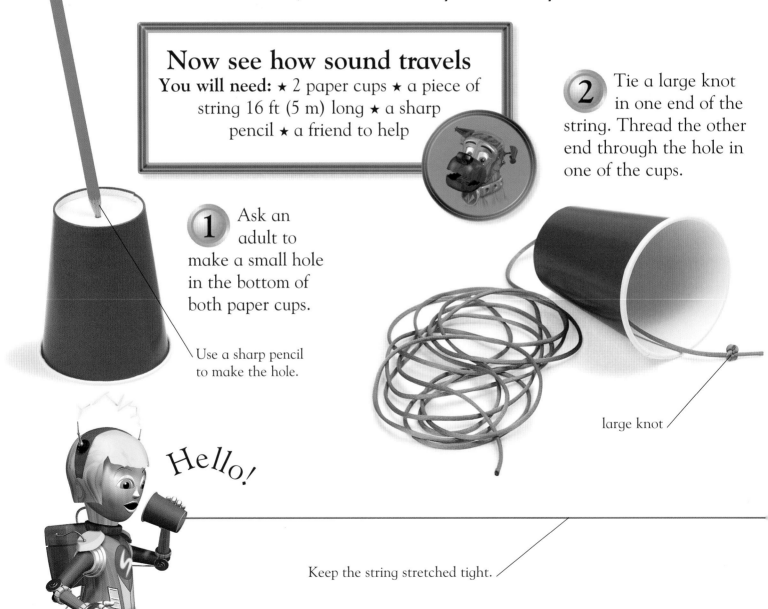

Now see how sound travels
You will need: ★ 2 paper cups ★ a piece of string 16 ft (5 m) long ★ a sharp pencil ★ a friend to help

1 Ask an adult to make a small hole in the bottom of both paper cups.

Use a sharp pencil to make the hole.

2 Tie a large knot in one end of the string. Thread the other end through the hole in one of the cups.

large knot

Hello!

Keep the string stretched tight.

A beating heart

A doctor can listen to your heartbeat using an instrument called a stethoscope. The end of the stethoscope is pressed against your chest. The quiet sounds of your heart beating travel through the tubes to the doctor's ears.

Science explained

When you speak into the string telephone, the sound of your voice bounces around inside the cup. This makes the string shake or vibrate. The string must be stretched tight, otherwise the vibrations cannot travel along it to the person listening at the other end.

This is your string telephone.

The string threads between the cups.

3 Thread the end of the string without the knot through the hole in the other cup. Now tie a large knot.

4 Hold the telephone with your friend, like Chip and Pixel are doing. Ask your friend to talk into his or her cup. Hold your cup to your ear. Can you hear what your friend is saying?

Hello!

Stand about 16 ft (5 m) apart.

Block out sounds

Some materials stop sound waves from bouncing around. They can help make loud sounds quieter or block out unpleasant noises. Using materials to block out noise is called soundproofing.

Crash

Make a soundproof box
You will need: ★ an alarm clock ★ a cardboard box ★ wrapping paper or old newspaper ★ bubble wrap or several layers of plastic ★ a small towel

1 Set the alarm clock ringing, and put it inside the box. Put on the lid. Can you still hear the alarm clock ringing?

2 Next, wrap the ringing clock in some wrapping paper, and put it inside the box again. Does the paper make the ringing quieter?

Science explained

The ringing sound of an alarm clock travels easily through air and hard, smooth materials, such as cardboard. Softer materials, such as bubble wrap and fabric, stop the sound waves from bouncing around. They soundproof the noise by making the ringing sound quieter.

Hearing protectors

Some noises are so loud that they hurt your ears. It is important to avoid very loud sounds. The ground crew who help to park the planes at airports wear special soundproof hearing protectors. These protect their ears from the loud engine noises.

3 Take off the wrapping paper. Cover the ringing clock in bubble wrap, and put it inside the box. How loud is the ringing now?

4 Now wrap the ringing clock in the paper, bubble wrap, and a towel. Do these materials and the box soundproof the ringing?

It's quiz time!

Now that you have completed the experiments, have fun testing your knowledge of sound and music. Look back for help if you are unsure of any of the answers.

Let's go!

Can you find what doesn't belong?
Look at the lists of words below. Can you figure out which word in each line is unlike the others?

1 pluck   bang   eat   blow

2 moving   singing   barking   shouting

3 drum   chimes   guitar   book

Can you choose the correct words?
Look at each sentence below. Choose which one of the three shaded words makes the sentence true.

How's it going?

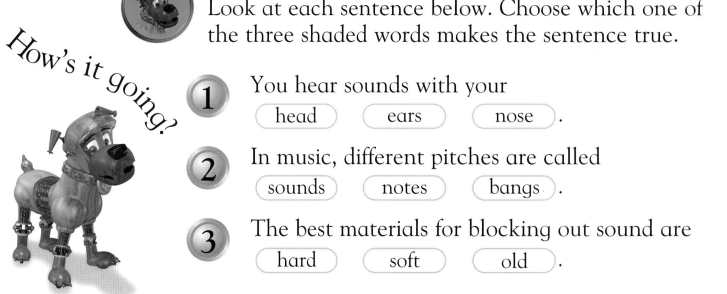

1 You hear sounds with your
(head)   (ears)   (nose).

2 In music, different pitches are called
(sounds)   (notes)   (bangs).

3 The best materials for blocking out sound are
(hard)   (soft)   (old).

What's going on?

Can you answer the questions below?

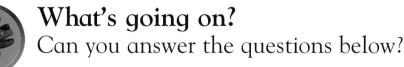

1 Why can't Newton hear Pixel making a noise?

2 Chip is talking into a bucket. What can he hear?

3 Pixel is holding a tube up to one ear. Can she figure out where on the tube Newton is tapping?

Now check your answers.

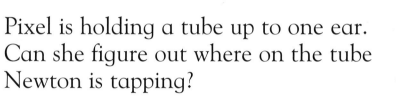

Give yourself one point for each correct answer.

Well done!
More than **3 points**

Very good!!
More than **5 points**

Brilliant!!!
More than **8 points**

What's going on?

1 Newton has covered up his ears with a soundproof material so he can't hear Pixel making a noise.

2 Chip can hear an echo of his voice in the bucket.

3 It's difficult for Pixel to figure out where Newton is tapping because she is only listening with one ear, not two.

Choose the correct words

1 Ears

2 Notes

3 Soft

What doesn't belong?

1 Eat – the other words describe what you can do to musical instruments to make sounds.

2 Moving – the other words are types of sound.

3 Book – all the others are musical instruments.

Glossary

Amplify
To amplify a sound is to make it louder.

Battery
A battery is an electrical part filled with special chemicals. These chemicals make electricity flow when the battery is connected in a complete circuit.

Beam
A beam is a bright disc of light that travels in a straight line from a light source. Flashlights and spotlights make beams of light.

Bend
To bend something is to use a force to change its shape from straight to curved. You can, for example, bend a straight straw to make it into a curved shape.

Bulb
A bulb is an electrical part that lights up when it is connected in a complete circuit with a battery.

Buzzer
A buzzer is an electrical part that makes a buzzing sound when it is connected in a complete circuit with a battery.

Circuit
A circuit is a ring, or loop, of wires and electrical parts. A circuit must be in a continuous loop, without any breaks, for the electrical parts to work.

Color
Red, orange, yellow, green, blue, indigo, and violet are colors. You can see these colors in a rainbow. You can make thousands more colors and shades by mixing together different colored lights or paints.

Conductor
A conductor is a material that electricity can pass through. Metal objects, such as metal spoons, keys, and metal paper clips, are all conductors of electricity.

Dark

Darkness is the absence of light.
You cannot see easily in the dark.

Direction

An object's direction describes where it is going. A car, for example, can move in a forward or backward direction.

Disconnect

If you disconnect something you break the circuit and stop electricity moving.

Ear

You hear sounds with your ears.
An ear is specially shaped to collect sound waves that travel through the air.

Echo

An echo is a sound that has bounced off a hard surface. You can hear an echo if you make a loud noise inside a cave. The sound bounces back to your ears.

Electricity

Electricity is a form of energy that can be used to produce light, heat, and to make machines work. It can be dangerous; ask permission before you use electrical items.

Fluorescent

This describes brightly colored materials that show up, or reflect, light very well.

Force

A force is a push or a pull. Forces can make an object change its shape, speed, or direction. Pushing a merry-go-round to speed it up is an example of a force.

Friction

Friction is the force that slows down an object when it slides over something else. The more friction there is, the more the object slows down. Carpet, for example, makes more friction than vinyl, and so a toy car slows down more quickly on carpet than on vinyl.

Hearing

Hearing is one of your five senses.
It is the sense that makes you aware of sound, such as the sound of music playing on the radio. You use both of your ears to hear.

Image

An image can be a picture, photograph, or statue. The pictures you see at the movie theater and on a television screen are images made with light.

Insulator

An insulator is a material that electricity cannot pass through. Plastic and wood are both insulators of electricity.

Light

Light comes from the Sun, electric lights, and fire. You need light to see things. Light is made up of different colors.

Light source

A light source gives out light. The Sun, a flashlight, and a lamp are examples of different light sources.

Electricity

Household current is a powerful form of electricity. It travels in wires from power stations to our homes. Never experiment or play with electricity; it is dangerous, and you could get an electric shock.

Megaphone

A megaphone is a cone-shaped object that makes it possible for people to hear you from far away when you speak into it.

Microphone

A microphone changes a sound into electricity so that it can be amplified. Microphones are often used by singers.

Mirror

A mirror is a smooth piece of glass or shiny metal that reflects light.

Motor

A motor is an electrical part with a spindle that spins around when the motor is connected in a complete circuit with a battery.

Move

When something moves, it changes its place or position. You can move from one place to another by walking, running, or jumping.

Music

Music is the sound made by people singing or playing instruments.

Noise

A noise is a sound. We often call an unpleasant sound a noise. An example of a noise is the sound of a construction worker using a jackhammer.

Note

In music, different pitched sounds are called notes. For example, when a musician plays a guitar, the notes are made by plucking the strings.

Percussion

This word describes instruments, such as drums or chimes, that you tap or strike to make a musical sound.

Pitch

The pitch of a sound is how high or low it is. A sound, such as a whistle, has a high pitch. A sound, such as a rumble of thunder, has a low pitch.

Plug

A plug connects an electrical item to the household electricity. Never touch a plug or turn anything on or off without permission; you could get an electric shock.

Power station

A power station is a factory where huge machines make electricity and send it to our homes through wires.

Primary colors

The three primary colors for paint are red, yellow, and blue. These are the colors that, when mixed together in different amounts, make other colors. Mixing red and yellow makes orange; mixing red and blue makes purple; and mixing blue and yellow makes green.

Pull

A pull is a type of force, such as a stretch. When you pull something, such as a door, you move it toward yourself. The opposite of a pull is a push.

Push

A push is a type of force, such as a kick or a blow. When you push something, such as a door, you move it away from yourself. The opposite of a push is a pull.

Rainbow

A rainbow is a band of colors (red, orange, yellow, green, blue, indigo, and violet) that make up sunlight.

Reflect

To reflect is to mirror, or to throw back from a surface, like a ball bouncing off a wall.

Reflection

You see your reflection when you look into a mirror, or into a window, or into still water.

Rhythm

This is a repeated pattern of sound.

Roll

To move by turning around and around or over and over, like a stone rolling down a hill or the wheels on a bicycle.

Shadow

A shadow is the dark area behind a solid object when that object has blocked out the light. On a sunny day, buildings and objects cast dark shadows.

Socket

A socket, or electrical outlet, is a place where the plug on an electrical item can be connected to the household electricity. Never touch a socket; you could get an electric shock.

Sound

Anything you hear is a sound. Waves of sound travel through the air from the source of the sound to your ears.

Soundproof

When an object or a material is soundproof, sound cannot pass through it. Musicians often practice in rooms that are soundproof so they don't disturb other people.

Sound waves

These are invisible ripples of sound that move through the air.

Speed

This is how fast something is moving.

Squash

To squash something is to push, or press on it, so that it changes its shape and size.

Squeeze

To squeeze something is to press or crush it. You can get the juice out of a lemon by squeezing it.

Stretch

To stretch something is to pull it so that it becomes longer.

Sun

The Sun is our nearest star. It gives out massive amounts of light. You must never look directly at the Sun – it could seriously damage your eyes.

Sunlight

This is the light that comes from the Sun.

Switch

A switch is an electrical part that opens or closes a break in a circuit, turning it on and off. Never touch a switch with wet hands; you could get an electric shock.

Tracking

When you track something you try to follow its path. You track sounds with both of your ears.

Transparent

Something that is transparent or see-through lets light pass through it. Glass and some plastics are transparent materials.

Twist

To twist something is to use pushes and pulls to turn different parts of an object in different directions.

Vibration

If you twang, bang, or rattle musical instruments, they make quick shaking movements, or vibrations that produce sound waves in the air.

White light

Light from the Sun is white. White light is a mixture of all seven colors of the rainbow.

Wire

A wire is a long, thin piece of metal that carries electricity around a circuit. It is often covered in plastic to protect people from electric shocks.

Index

Bye-bye!

125

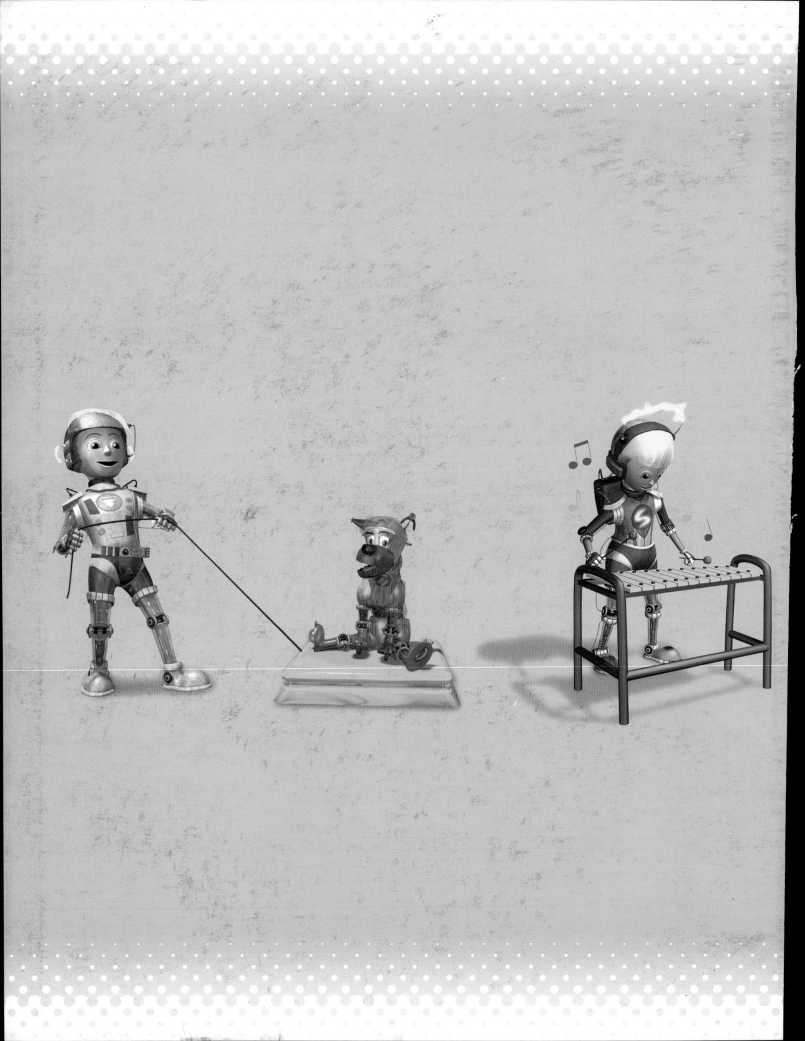